The Witness
to
Hollywood and Heaven

Pamela Sherrod

ISBN: 0-6155-7636-2
ISBN-13: 9780615576367

Miracles and Angels Publications
A Division of
Pamela Sherrod Ministries
P.O. Box 53371
Sarasota, Florida 34232

www.pamelasherrodministries.org
www.miraclesandangels.org

Scripture quotations:
Scripture taken from the HOLY BIBLE, NEW INTERNATIONAL VERSION
® Copyright © 1973, 978, 1984 by International Bible Society. Used by
permission of Zondervan. All rights reserved.

Dedication

This book is dedicated to my daughter, Sandra, with prayers that she'll always remember the miracles witnessed, as she, herself, was one of the most wonderful wonders of all.

Table of Contents

Prologue

I am a witness to the amazing miracles that prove that God is real! I'm a witness to the fact that, through Christ, there is eternal life. When I lost my fiancé, God was merciful in assuring me that he'd ascended into heaven. The Lord offered me a visit with him and blessed my life with a revelation that was astonishing. I'd known that I was on a spiritual journey, but never imagined that there was a 'route' to heaven and back.

This is **your** invitation to begin your own life-changing journey, and a prayer that you'll experience similar miracles!

Introduction

It would take at least a year to document all the wondrous things I've seen, but in this book I'm pleased to share the most amazing experiences I've had, thus far. During my lifetime, I've stumbled into situations that have led to, both, horrific tragedies and magnificent revelations. Some have asked, "How can you, after knowing so much adversity, still believe in a loving Savior?" I have to admit, it's not entirely by faith. I've actually seen Jesus, experienced his presence and captured a glimpse of the heaven he's promised us.

In 2009, I lost my two closest partners within only thirty-five days and thought that my life had crumbled. Suddenly, without warning, four years of hard work and beautiful dreams had ended. One was my writing partner and the wife of a famous Rat Pack star. The other was my fiancé, a former alcoholic who'd given his life to Christ. I'd later realize that, with one, I'd witnessed some of the darkest secrets hidden behind Hollywood's most glamorous lives. With the other, I witnessed proof of the existence of the afterlife, and one of the greatest secrets surrounding our access to heaven. The latter would be a life-changing event, for it opened my eyes to the amazing mysteries tucked quietly in the Bible.

I was initially torn when it came to revealing this story. I considered it a personal and sacred experience, and a blessing that I, alone, would cherish. Although I gained great joy from learning about the miracles of other believers and created a website on which to share them, I still remained silent about my own. I was so astonished by what I'd seen that I could scarcely find the words to explain it. Lacking a degree in theology, I also harbored a deep fear that, if I actually offered my testimony, people would question its validity, or worse, my sanity. Who was I, anyway, that the Lord would reveal such things?

God, however, has a way of dealing with us when we're governed by fear. He made it known that, as a witness to his miracles I had a responsibility to testify to the nature of his grace. I'd often asked, "Why me?" But, I began to realize how selfish this was. There's a specific reason why each of us is called to a specific task. In the same way that a believer who's overcome drug abuse can offer valuable guidance to a struggling addict, my troubled past and painful experiences have made me more sensitive to the pain felt by others. Many people suffer each year from devastating losses and shattered lives, and it's my prayer that I can offer some degree of comfort by sharing my experience and the miracles I witnessed.

God really exists. If he didn't, I wouldn't have survived to actually document these events. I faced brutal realities that had shaken my world, staggering defeats that had clouded my dreams. I was crushed by pressures that came from every direction and knew the paralyzing fear of what awaited me in the future. For over forty years, I'd battled with severe arthritis and numerous surgeries, and they'd turned my financial and personal life into a virtual roller-coaster. Then, the wind was taken from my sails when a valuable screenplay was stolen, an injustice that left me with a deep sense of powerlessness. I watched, as the greed of Hollywood vultures preyed on what was left of my writing partner's life. Then, when my fiancé died, mistakenly believing that I was leaving him, I lived with the inconsolable grief that follows a tragic and shocking death. It was along this dark and jagged journey, when I had nothing left but my faith to hold onto, that I desperately searched for God's answers. The Lord, with his merciful love, answered my prayers. Then, he blessed me with a series of miracles, far beyond anything I thought was possible.

I've had the indescribable joy of feeling the Lord's presence in a deep and personal way. I was given a glimpse of heaven and I learned that, through Christ all things are truly possible, even a spiritual connection to our loved ones who've departed. Without a doubt, I know that the promise of eternity is real, and that through our Lord, Jesus Christ, we have access to it.

In our culture, we're torn by an ever-growing list of pressures and demands. However, when a crisis develops and our lives are disrupted, we're often forced to make a decision. We can either run to the Lord for strength and comfort, or turn away. Many people, even believers, struggle with their faith during difficult times. They wonder if their prayers are actually heard. Or wonder if God has suddenly forsaken them.

I've known and wrestled with both of these feelings. During the darkest of periods, however, I've urgently prayed for direction, hoping that God would fulfill the promises in the Scriptures and restore my life. When I look back now, I realize that he did much more than that. He actually gave me a new one.

I initially released this testimony in 2011 to offer hope and comfort to those who're going through difficult times. I planned to eventually publish it, but I first presented the story as a free gift during the holiday season. During the following spring, however, I began to hesitate, stewing over questions about what to say. Could I actually guarantee that believers could visit heaven? Or promise a grieving husband that he'd see his wife? I didn't have the authority to proclaim these promises, but I could offer proof from my own experiences that these things were truly possible.

I was also concerned about another matter. Years before, I'd heard God's spirit say, "Tell the children to stay away from the occult." I still needed to deliver this message and warn adults, as well as children, to avoid dabbling in this activity. This would be hard for some to accept, especially those grieving from the loss of a loved one. But, no matter how much we may miss those who've left us, we shouldn't try to reach them through the use of the occult.

Years before, I'd never known why I received this message. After seeing heaven, however, and experiencing God's miracles, I began to understand the reason. The Lord was, and is, the only source that we should turn to. Jesus knows what our needs are, and through the power of the Holy Spirit, our needs will be met. Still, I wondered, if readers reached out to Jesus, would he present himself in the same powerful manner in which I'd witnessed his grace? I prayed for answers, because I couldn't confidently share my story without being assured that he would 'back me up.'

Six months passed and I still hadn't published the book and I'd given myself plenty of excuses. However, my foot-dragging days would be brought to an end. During a month in which my life turned completely upside-down, it was obvious that I had to stop procrastinating. It was time to get started. My prayers became more urgent as I desperately needed a confirmation of my role.

In the following three weeks, the Lord, in his merciful manner, sent the 'green light' that I needed in six magnificent messages. The first came when I accidently tuned into a televised sermon presented by Pastor Keith Moore. His testimony was unforgettable and I cried with joy after hearing it.

Following his father's death, Pastor Moore had an experience which was similar to mine. His father's loss had hit him very hard. However, during a powerful vision, he was blessed with the opportunity to visit his dad in a realm that he recognized as heaven. Still, like many of us, he kept silent about the experience for several years. Then, the night before his sermon, he felt moved by the Lord to finally share this blessing. In fact, Pastor Moore urged other Christians to reach out and share their own. God had healed our hearts with his comforting love, but not merely for our benefit, but for others. We were meant to share the miracles we'd witnessed with those who were suffering. This event would reconfirm a message I'd read in Isaiah 43:12 that said: *"I have revealed and saved and proclaimed–I, and not some foreign god among you. You are my witnesses,"* declares the LORD, *"that I am God."*

This, along with the other five messages, made it clear that God was speaking to me. It was the last one, however, that convinced me that it was time to 'step out' and take action.

During a service at Sarasota, Florida's Church of Hope, Pastor Scott Young said that we're often called by God to do something that we're not sure we're worthy of, but that God will handle what we can't naturally accomplish on our own. He stressed that, when the Lord has given you a mission, hiding in the crowd is not an option. We have to take risks and step forward, trusting in God to make a way for us.

At that moment, I realized that I was ready, just as I was, broken and imperfect, but chosen for a specific purpose. So, on Sunday afternoon, on September 9, 2012, I prayed in church and took the steps to move forward.

I'm pleased to be a 'witness' to the fact that God is real, and to offer this, my testimony of his magnificent miracles.

-Pamela Sherrod

Chapter One: In The Beginning

In the beginning God created the heavens and the earth.
Genesis 1:1

I didn't realize the significance of these words until I recently sat down to reflect on my life. That's because, prior to April 2009, I didn't seriously think about experiencing anything in heaven, at least, not until it was "my time to go." My outlook radically changed, however, when my two closest partners tragically died only thirty-five days apart, bringing all of our dreams to a halt. One was Altovise, the widow of the famous Rat Pack star, Sammy Davis, Jr. She was my writing partner and co-founder of our publishing and production company. The other was my fiancé, an aspiring writer who was relatively unknown outside his circle of friends. Looking back, I realized that they shared not only a fatal attraction to alcohol, but a loss of hope in ever regaining their former lifestyles.

Shocked by their deaths, I plunged into a season of writing, determined to complete the work I'd begun with Altovise. A trained journalist, I felt obligated to disclose all of the Hollywood drama we'd experienced. I was driven by an obsession to chronicle each and every horror. After all, I'd been a key witness in a lawsuit blocking a movie about Sammy's life, and the behind-the-scenes corruption that had played the starring role. Much of Altovise's life had been dragged through the mud and scandalized. Wasn't I obligated to tell her side of the story? Wasn't that why we'd been introduced? And shouldn't I stand up for justice, even for myself? Who else would disclose the sordid details surrounding our 'borrowed' screenplay? Who'd finally present the story we'd created?

Yes, I felt proud to have summoned the courage to speak out, even confront the entertainment field's most powerful company. So, fueled by dark and inescapable memories, I put my energy into publishing *The Last Chapter in the Life of Mrs. Sammy Davis, Jr.*, and our screenplay, *A Detour to Mexico*. The material was controversial, but in the spring of 2011, with both projects finished, I felt like I'd accomplished something worthy. I'd defied all the tragedies, setbacks, and the fear of repercussions to publish an insider's view of Hollywood. What could be more compelling?

"Stop!" was the word I heard, however, just days after publishing *A Detour to Mexico,* and a split second before my fan shut down, and all the power in the house. What had caused the outage? There was no storm, no rumble of thunder, not even a breeze. Someone else may have thought it was coincidental, but I knew it wasn't. I'd experienced many similar 'coincidences,' and recognized the signs. During that uncomfortable silence, I reflected on one of the first times I'd heard that unfaltering 'voice.'

I'd never spoken of it, and carefully omitted it from my books, but while reading the Bible one night, I heard in a very forceful message: "Tell the children to stay away from the occult."

It was striking, because the words came from something other than a voice, and yet, it was distinctly heard. I hadn't formed the message, and yet, it came from somewhere within me. Odder still, was the fact that I knew very little about the occult and wasn't even sure of what it consisted of.

My education began the following day, when I happened to visit a friend's church, and the minister launched into a forty-minute sermon on the dangers of the occult.

"Wow," I murmured. "Is he reading my mind?"

He offered, not only a detailed list of everything that fell under this category, but advice on how to identify it.

If that wasn't surprising enough, during the following week, I had an over-the-phone-meeting with a small, independent producer who'd contacted me to write a new T.V. show for kids. I was delighted, and couldn't wait to hear the details and begin working on the proposal and sample episodes.

"Great!" I kept saying. "Let's do it!"

It seemed like a dream-come-true, a job that would lead back to television, where I'd once before worked. I wanted to be involved in ministry work, but felt that I could do both. Just before hanging up, he urged me to rent a Harry Potter movie, so I'd have a feel for the format.

"Sure," I said. "No problem."

There was a problem. I played the movie, and within less than three minutes, I knew I was in trouble. The scene opened to witches casting spells and incantations in an ominous-looking setting that immediately triggered an alarm. Although the T.V. was still on, my mind raced back to the message I'd heard: "Tell the children to stay away from the occult."

I silenced the T.V. and flopped down in a chair. What a disaster, I thought. An invisible foot had slammed on the brakes, and my dream career had just hit the windshield. There was no way that I could take the assignment. It involved doing the exact opposite of what God had called me to do. In fact, I believed that my mission was to share stories about his miracles.

So, I prayed hard before calling the producer, hoping God would somehow intervene. Surely, there was another way around this issue, another deal that we could strike.

"Please God!" I pleaded. "Isn't there something I can do?"

When I finally called, I didn't mention the 'voice message' I'd heard. He'd think I was crazy. Instead, I said that my spiritual beliefs prevented me from promoting the occult, and asked if they'd consider a different approach. I suggested a show surrounding "the cutest teen angels on T.V." I'd gotten the idea at a Christian Women's meeting, when I noticed a friend's pen was framed like an angel. I believed it was a divine answer–an open window in a burning house–and so I presented it. After talking it over with his partner, the producer called back and said they liked the concept, and gave me the green light to go ahead. I was ecstatic. Suddenly, I was back in the driver's seat. I consulted an old friend who was a writer/producer at the Disney Channel, and he offered valuable tips, resources and materials to study. I read the latest books on screenwriting and learned how to develop engaging plots and characters, but despite the fact that I worked around the clock and delivered the entire project on time, the producer never paid for the finished package.

"We're sending it," he claimed, about the check that never came. It was a very blunt message to a naïve screenwriter who'd worked without a written contract: "Welcome to Hollywood!"

Yes, I'd definitely heard that 'voice' before. It seemed to come at pivotal points in my life, and I'd always wondered, "Why me?" After all, I was a single mother, struggling with health issues and financial problems. Didn't God appreciate my situation? How could he ask these things of me?

Even before I'd first heard the voice, there had been messages of a different nature. They were spiritual encounters which I still didn't understand. For example, an amazing occurrence took place in an apostolic church in Connecticut. It was there that I confronted my deepest doubts about the Holy Spirit. It was also where I began to step into a spiritual realm that I never knew existed. I documented some of these experiences in my first book, **Crossing the Burning Sands,** which included this excerpt:

There was a woman on my right whose mouth was trembling uncontrollably and, as though in a trance, she uttered incomprehensible sounds. The pastor was lying prostrate on the floor, tears flowing from his eyes as he, too, spoke in tongues. His mother was suddenly reared backwards in her chair, nearly flipping over completely. I turned toward Glenda, who was worshiping and crying out loudly. Everyone seemed to be experiencing a presence that had entered the room, except for me, whom the Spirit had apparently jumped right over.

I'd long had deep suspicions about phony preachers and grinning hypocrites. I disliked their undignified performances. I'd grimaced when I thought of congregations that allowed themselves to be worked up into senseless frenzies, unable to distinguish between what was genuine and what was contrived. Yet, here I was, praying for the "real" Spirit to show up. Would it come? Suddenly, I was confronted with an arresting thought. How would I respond if, and when, the Spirit actually filled me?

I put my hands over my face and continued to pray. I was concentrating as hard as I could, trying to feel God's presence. Then, in a vision that slowly evolved, I saw a narrow path, which led through an undeveloped land. Was it somewhere in the Middle East? I wondered. Or, was it simply something I'd recalled from an old movie? Somehow, the vision led me along the outskirts of an old town and I suddenly believed that I was seeing a path that Jesus had walked. I continued to follow the route with my eyes, wondering when I was going to feel something significant.

Then, I was in darkness, again, and the faces of old men of age began to flash before me. Many of them were heavily bearded and their eyes were full of quiet wisdom. They were staring at me, yet their faces were expressionless. I didn't know who they were, but I sensed that none of them was Jesus.

Moments later, Glenda tapped me on my arm and began to say something, only I couldn't hear her voice. In fact, her voice seemed to be coming from a remote place, as though she were standing in a far-away tunnel. Alarmed, I immediately grabbed her hand and tried to let her know that something was wrong. But when I opened my mouth, I could barely hear my own voice. My words came from so far away that it felt like I was having an out-of-body experience. It was like those last fleeting seconds of consciousness before surgery, when the anesthesia takes effect, and everyone's face and voice fades into the distance.

"Glenda!" I uttered, trying to scream, "I can't hear you...I can't hear myself!"

The Spirit had come.

Timothy later assured me that I hadn't been hallucinating. He and his wife seemed completely unmoved when we spoke about what had transpired; in fact, they said that it was a common occurrence.

"Common?" I thought, still shaken. That was not my idea of an ordinary service.

"That's the way he sometimes approaches you," Timothy said. "He's too much of a gentleman to come to you forcefully. He's a gentle Spirit."

Increasingly, I felt the presence of this loving Spirit in my life. Maybe, it had always been there, because when I was young I wanted to be a nun and to live close to the Lord. My mother, however, reminded me that I wasn't Catholic, so I needed to look for another mission.

Years later, I developed slipped capital femoral epiphysis in both of my hips. While, surgical procedures in recent years have been extraordinary in helping patients regain their mobility, back in the early 1970's, this wasn't always the case. After a number of unsuccessful surgeries, I was left with painful arthritis and physical limitations that would impact even my ability to be intimate in a future marriage or relationship. The reality was very sobering, and it made me wonder about my role and my value as a woman. Was I to live a different life for God's purpose? Throughout the years, I'd tussle over this question, alternating between efforts to live my own life, and the calling to submit to God's will.

In many ways, it felt as though the Lord was guiding me through a special journey. Often, when I'd opened the Scriptures, I felt 'led' to specific passages. I'd ask a question, or pray about an issue, and without fail, the book would open to a stunning answer. After nearly thirty years, I no longer called these occurrences 'coincidences.' Nor the occasions when I'd had strange dreams that preceded similar events.

During one of these dreams, I envisioned a car trip that I was taking with my mother, when a plane suddenly landed near us on the highway. When I awoke the following morning, I learned that a small aircraft had made an emergency landing on Interstate 95, in the neighboring town of Stratford, Connecticut.

Then, in 1983, while working as a T.V. Desk Assistant at ABC News, I had a nightmare about a hostage situation which required that the doors to the newsroom be locked–something that was only done during an emergency. Three days later, a gunman took the bureau hostage, threatening to blow it up unless he was allowed to speak with our anchorman on the air. He'd taken one of our security guards at gunpoint, and was hiding somewhere in the bureau. The late Peter Jennings was hosting the show that night, and the producers decided to go forward with the broadcast but make no deals with the gunman. Although the building was evacuated, I stayed to help the editors and producers of *World News Tonight*. Police officers filled the building, and a helicopter circled above it.

When Peter and the producers were safely in the newsroom, the doors were immediately locked.

Several other news agencies covered the crisis. Peter, however, didn't mention it until the end of the broadcast, moments after the gunman had given himself up. I waited even longer before briefing my parents–trying to protect them from unnecessary worries. I never spoke (or wrote) about the dream, however, as I also wanted to protect my career. Two weeks later, after being thanked by the bureau chief, I was assigned to my first show, *Nightline*.

As the years passed, these strange dreams and occurrences became more frequent. Being a journalist, I recorded them in nearly seventy journals. Some incidents would stand out in my memory more than others, like the day when I had a vision of disabled people being healed in a church, and when I stood up, I was completely free of my own arthritic pain for over twenty-four hours.

In 1996, after praying for years to have a child, I had a dream about delivering a baby girl and was 'led' to a message in Isaiah 54 which seemed to confirm the vision. Coincidentally, that week, a relative also heard that same scripture cited on a Christian radio program and believed it was meant for me. About a year later, I'd have another powerful dream about a child.

The guy I was dating, however, tried to discourage the idea. I was nearly forty and had already had eight hip surgeries, including two for artificial hip replacements. In his opinion, I was too old and too unhealthy to even think of conceiving a child. He believed that, since I was married when I was younger, but never had children, I probably wasn't able to.

"I have a seventeen-year old," he boasted, " ...so I'm not the one with the problem."

He suggested that, after we married we could look into adaption. Besides, he stressed, "Only poor, uneducated people in old religious communities believe in miracles." Since we'd both once worked for ABC, surely we were above such nonsense. He laughed and said, "It's always some poor girl in southern France, or somewhere, who's seen a miracle."

Suddenly, the film, **The Song of Bernadette,** came to mind, but I kept this to myself.

Despite my U.S. citizenship, an amazing series of events unfolded. During the tumultuous seasons that followed, there would be brutal physical trials and challenges to my health, but about two years later, I'd finally hold my 'miracle baby' in my arms.

The celebration was bitter-sweet. Two weeks later, I was rushed back to the hospital, fighting for my life. I suffered from partially obstructed intestines, a condition accompanied by excruciating abdominal pain. Eating was impossible, since no food would stay down. Walking was painful and I was dependent upon crutches, because my artificial hips were collapsing. Thoughts of reconstructive surgery had to wait, because one of the six huge fibroid tumors that had threatened my pregnancy was still pressed against my bladder. If all that wasn't enough, the arthritis which had plagued my hips for decades had now spread to my spine and ankles.

Multiple surgeries were needed, but I was too weak to endure any of them. In the midst of the crisis, I saw the strange irony of it all. My life had been full of painful struggles, but for the first time, I had something that made it worthwhile–a child to love. I was so ill, however, that without a miracle, I didn't believe I'd leave the hospital alive. During those desperate moments, I read a wonderful scripture and it guided me, in terms of the words that I should pray. Within the following ten minutes, I vowed to serve God for the rest of my life, and then dedicated my child to him.

Miraculously, I began to recover the following day. When I left the hospital, I knew that I was married to Christ, and interpreted it to mean that I'd accept a life of celibacy and seek a role in the ministry. Since I'd wanted to be a nun when I was young, in an odd way, I'd been given my wish. For the following eight years, I honored this vow with no complications.

That's how it all began.

Much of this was recorded in *Crossing the Burning Sands*, a manuscript which took nearly fifteen years to write. The delay was mostly due to fears about recording the miracles I'd seen. In the first chapters, I actually refrained from mentioning them at all. However, by the time I reached the middle, they were impossible to omit. How could I ignore a reality that, like the changing seasons, was part of my life? The problem was, I didn't know how to record them. If I disclosed too much, there was the danger of frightening readers. On the flip side, if I revealed too little, there was the risk of trivializing events that were more important than I realized. And how would I handle the likely questions? What type of phenomena was it, anyway? Did I even have the courage to find out? I wasn't sure, but I couldn't continue to cover it up.

When the manuscript was finally finished, I was still torn about how to handle it. I prayed every day, studied the Bible and recorded church sermons in my journals, but I was increasingly confused about the nature of my ministry. At various times, I thought that God was telling me to "build his house," and although I'd never wanted to live in Alabama, I started buying my grandparents' land there to develop a church. Was that what he wanted? I wasn't completely sure, but I had to raise the money, one way or another.

When I was asked to help Altovise Davis write her autobiography, I quickly jumped at the opportunity, thinking I'd raise the money through our collaboration. But, had I jumped in over my head? While friends thought that my life had been tumultuous, no one could have imagined what was still ahead. A partnership that initially promised to be star-studded with the glamour that emanated from the Rat Pack's fame, would eventually lead to a heartbreaking season of multiple tragedies.

I shared many of these experiences in *The Last Chapter in the Life of Mrs. Sammy Davis, Jr.*, but, it was only while taping a radio talk show that a crucial point would finally hit me. It was the significance of the word 'witness.' I was talking about Hollywood, and how I'd been a witness in a lawsuit blocking a film about Sammy, when something powerful struck me.

Pamela Ann Sherrod

It was a flashback to a scripture I'd read in Isaiah 43 about being a witness:

"Which of them foretold this and proclaimed to us the former things? ...You are my witnesses," declares the LORD, "and my servant whom I have chosen, so that you may know and believe me and understand that I am he ...You are my witnesses," declares the Lord, "that I am God."

I recalled these words because I was actually 'led' to this message on two remarkable occasions. The first time was on February 4, 2006. I'd initially thought it was coincidental that the verses contained a reference to Egypt. On that same morning, I'd read about the mysterious circumstances surrounding an Egyptian cruise ship that sank with few survivors.

Then, years later, I'd stumble upon the scripture, again, only an hour after hearing of the first Egyptian casualties in their country's political uprising. As I picked up my journal to make a note, I happened to glance at my calendar. I was stunned. It was February 4, 2011, exactly five years after I'd first read that passage and recorded the date in my Bible.

Could these dates and events have been coincidental? Or, did they hold some special significance? Hadn't it been five years since I'd shifted my focus from being a witness for Christ to being a witness to the troublesome events in Hollywood? Had I allowed that much time to slip by?

I'd experienced extraordinary encounters, especially with Altovise. However, the most important things that I'd seen were the miracles that God had revealed.

So, why hadn't I shared them?

Was I was lured by the glamour of Tinseltown? Had I fallen into the same trap that kept millions focused on empty images? Hollywood offered a magical escape from reality—with all of its trials and pressures—and its producers were good at creating illusions of heaven-on-earth. But, despite the extravagant sets and special effects, glorious scenes and beautiful faces, they couldn't replicate the real nature of heaven, nor fill the void that stemmed from most people's desire to experience it. Only God could.

I'd been a witness to God's amazing miracles and the eternal realm offered to us through Christ. Suddenly, I began to understand why I'd been reminded of the powerful message in Isaiah 43.

Chapter Two: Stop

"Be still and know that I am God;
I will be exalted among the nations,
I will be exalted in the earth."
Psalm 46:10

When I heard the word "Stop" I knew that, like the biblical story of Jonah, I had to change my direction and deliver the testimony that I'd been given. For many years, I'd felt like I was hiding in silence. Even though I'd written books, I'd always been leery of sharing too many details about my 'supernatural' experiences, especially since I didn't fully understand them. How could I explain things that were still mysterious to me? After all, I wasn't an ordained minister.

I believed, however, that God was urging me to finally speak up and document them. I'd written extensively about my writing partner, Altovise Davis, but I'd mentioned almost nothing about my other partner, my fiancé. It was time to disclose the nature of his life, death and the miracle that unfolded afterward.

It began unexpectedly in church one Sunday morning. I'd attended many services across the country, and never expected to meet anyone there who'd challenge my spiritual views or conservative lifestyle. Certainly not at Harvest Tabernacle, which I considered the "outreach outpost" of downtown Sarasota. Yet, sitting beside me one day would be the first one.

He was a recovering alcoholic who'd been in and out of trouble, and believed he'd gotten a great deal when he traded his soul for the power of seduction. I never knew whether he'd been drunk and delusional or not, but he believed that he'd made an agreement with a demonic spirit and claimed that, since he'd made that devil's pact, his success rate with women had tripled. With the exception of drinking, his favorite pastime was actually cultivating ways to conquer them.

His name was Grover and he was extremely bright, and although he had a southern drawl that conjured images of an innocent 'country boy,' he was worldly in a dangerous sort of way. Articulate and well-read, he was particularly good at charming older women who were willing to lavish young men with expensive gifts. It seemed like a strange irony that I was then collaborating on a screenplay about a very similar gigolo.

Grover attended the Pentecostal services at the church, but only because he was enrolled in their rehab program. Even while there, he was outrageously flirtatious. No guy could upstage his bad-boy image, and for that, he was truly proud. Although he was attractive, it was his killer smile that charmed most women, along with his lewd sense of humor. I'd never known anyone who was so blatantly out of line.

Sophistication, in Grover's mind, meant that adults were mature enough to indulge in all of life's pleasures, no matter what the cost. Within only a few days, he'd decided that, with my puritanical views and modest lifestyle, I was the "most naïve person" he'd ever met. In his opinion, my intellectual level was also questionable, at best. I secretly laughed at his perceptions, amused by such a display of arrogance, especially by someone who was so unaccomplished.

Still, there were times when Grover could be endearing, and he was surprisingly entertaining. Within only one week of meeting him, I'd laughed more than in the previous ten years. While I often kept notes on the pastor's sermons, Grover had a habit of jotting down his own. Bored with church services, he would entertain himself by writing risqué notes. He loved to shock me, so when he passed me a folded paper, he'd always smirk as I read the unseemly message. In response, I'd scribble down a note about a scripture he should read, hoping it would curb his decadent thoughts. This was how our relationship began. It wasn't supposed to escalate to anything more than a humorous battle of the words and pens.

Perhaps it was our destiny to meet. We'd later wonder if the spiritual 'contracts' we'd made years before had somehow caused our paths to clash. For, as certainly as he'd struck a deal with the devil, I'd made my own covenant with God. During that first rocky season, we were like classic archenemies, but looking back, it seems like we were pulled into a battle that we didn't even understand. One thing, though, would become very clear. As our tug-of-war intensified, we'd both reveal our ulterior motives. I was as determined to save his rebellious soul as he was hell-bent on corrupting mine.

Thus, began a heated war, a passionate friendship, and an eternal love.

Four years later, I sat by Grover's hospital bed, and remembered those first challenging days and cried. How had we come to this point? Grover was in a coma, unable to speak, and I didn't even know what had caused his heart attack or seizure.

I cupped his hand in mine and whispered, "Grover, can you open your eyes?"

I desperately needed him to respond. If not, the physician was going to remove his life support.

"Grover, you've got to open your eyes!"

How did we get here? I wondered, somewhat dazed. What had happened to us?

I remembered the inner conflicts I'd had when our relationship began. I'd given my life to Christ, and was determined not to date anyone or wed again. I'd even backed out of my marriage plans to my daughter's father. I never expected a problem, because for eight years, I'd never had one. Whenever a guy expressed an interest in me, all I had to say was "I'm married to Christ," and they would run away–fast. So, why hadn't Grover run? Why, in fact, had he seemed more intrigued? I'd warned him that my life was not my own. Why did he always play with fire?

On the few occasions when I'd felt attracted to any man, I'd simply prayed that God would remove the feeling. And he always had. Grover was an entertaining distraction from all my problems, but since we were complete opposites, the thought of us being together seemed absurd. It was too farfetched to even imagine. So, I never expected any trouble.

Yet, one day, I realized that I was in trouble.

"God … " I prayed while driving. "Please, help me!" In a panic, I pulled the car to the side of the road, and put my head down. I wasn't supposed to become attached to Grover. It just wasn't supposed to happen.

"Please … take these feelings away!" I cried.

The feelings, however, only grew stronger.

I could write thick books about the years that followed. It was amazing, how two people, so unalike in every way, could become a loving couple. We both would change over time, but it was Grover's transformation that was most dramatic, and the striking evidence was first noticed when he gave his life to Christ and was baptized.

There were no other options for us, as a couple. I'd given my life to Christ, and in order to be with me, Grover had to give up his, as well. When I'd prayed about our relationship, I'd heard the 'voice' say, "No one comes to you but through me." So, I interpreted it to mean that Grover had to submit to the Lord, just as I had, before we could be married.

As with Altovise, I'd planned to eventually help Grover write his 'before-and-after' story. From his broken and troubled life would be an inspiring lesson about salvation. We both believed that his experience would prove that miracles still occurred. If God could redeem someone who'd literally sold his soul, it demonstrated that he could love and forgive anyone for their sins. And Grover, the prodigal son, was the perfect example.

I'd witnessed Grover's transformation up close. I saw a wayward, hard-drinking, womanizer reach for something higher when he turned toward the ministry. I also noticed that the younger men in the recovery programs looked up to him as a father figure, and it was soon apparent that he held great leadership potential. In fact, when he was promoted to an assistant director position, he quickly excelled in everything he handled. But, I cautioned him to wait until he'd grown closer to God and experienced the fullness of the Spirit, before assuming an official position. And he agreed that it was crucial to be authentic. Many of the guys were jaded and broken. They needed a leader whom they could trust, a man who truly walked with the Lord. So, he tried to prepare himself to offer them 'the real thing,' and not another let down.

After Grover's baptism, he still had a number of demons to fight and he suffered a few setbacks. He'd come a long way, though, and that, in itself, was a miracle. He prayed that he'd one day be a role model with a powerful testimony, and that he'd encourage other recovering addicts to put their trust in God.

I was Grover's biggest cheerleader, nurse and Bible teacher, and I intensely prayed for him every step of the way. His painful journey, however, was hard on both of us.

There was one point, in particular, when I'd almost given up. I'd had my tenth hip surgery, and was trying to get back on my feet when Grover lost his job and couldn't find another. His frustrations mounted, and his hopes began to plummet. Sinking in despair, he began a long drinking binge from which he never fully recovered. When his life spiraled out of control, I looked after him, though it was physically and emotionally draining. One day, I'd finally had enough of the backsliding, along with the cleanups required after his spoon feedings, vomiting and bedwetting. Alcoholism was ugly and I didn't have the strength to face any more of its horrors. But, just when I was about to call it quits, I'd had an unforgettable vision.

During those dreamlike moments, I saw a long dinner table prepared for an elaborate feast. There were several men already seated, and on the opposite side, near the end of the spread, was Jesus Christ. I was so excited to be in his company, that I started to take a seat. Just then, however, Jesus looked at me and asked without speaking, "Haven't you forgotten someone?" Instantly, I knew he was referring to Grover. So, I went back (to earth, presumably) and brought him back with me. In the dream, it seemed as though it took only a few seconds, but I couldn't judge how much time had actually passed. Only that Jesus was pleased.

"It's because of your love," Grover told me, " ... that I know that Jesus really exists." And he wanted to be the type of husband I'd be proud of. His heart was set on becoming a wholesome, godly man who was able to take care of his wife and family. This was the miracle that he was striving for and the core of his hopes for our future.

So, I was stunned by Grover's appearance on Easter Sunday, the last day that we'd talk. I'd enrolled him in a Christian rehab program located on an isolated farm, thinking it was ideal for him. However, he looked so aged and depressed during the church service, that I barely recognized him. I began to have second thoughts about the program. I'd hoped the peaceful setting would offer him a chance to draw closer to God, to nature, and the farm animals he'd always loved to tend. It took nearly two hours to reach it, though, and it may have been too far away.

Grover had agreed to go, but only for the sake of our engagement. I'd agreed to marry him, but only after he was healed of his addiction and he'd experienced the fullness of the Holy Spirit. For our marriage to be blessed, we both needed to be 'married to Christ.'

"Take care of him for me," I'd said to the directors, hoping I'd finally found a safe place for Grover. I had a lot of work to do. So, I took a deep breath, drove away, and turned my attention to my other partner–Altovise.

Mrs. Davis had spent a few seasons in Sarasota, where we were initially introduced to collaborate on her autobiography. Soon afterwards, however, we decided to write stories for children's books and films. We were on a mission to fulfill her husband's request.

Sammy Davis Jr.'s career began when he was only four, and since he'd never attended school, he couldn't read or write until he was an adult. He'd urged Altovise to stress to kids the importance of getting an education. We tried to do this with stories that inspired them to reach for higher goals. My strongest desire, though, was to share a special message about values and the miracle of love. Although our first screenplay, **A Detour to Mexico,** was believed to have been stolen, we'd decided to move forward. We'd wipe the dust off the manuscript and use it to launch our production company. Despite our initial setbacks, we were determined to publish and produce inspirational stories.

We'd just established Lil' SamHat Productions when disaster seemed to come from every direction. We learned of a scandalous book that had been released about Altovise and Sammy. It painted a very unsavory image of her.

Naturally, Altovise was upset, as it magnified the problems in an already stressful year. She was in a bitter lawsuit with her former partners, and the standoff had effectively blocked the negotiations on a movie deal about Sammy's life. It was just one of several setbacks and betrayals she'd endured. I was one of the witnesses in the case, and provided a lengthy deposition for her attorney. What I'd seen had tormented me. Swindlers seemed to prey on Altovise like vultures, and she realized that someone had raided her bank accounts, wiped out the stocks that Sammy had given her and helped themselves to many valuable keepsakes. The Presidential Ring that Sammy was presented by President Nixon was taken, as well as the priceless billfold given to him by actor, Richard Burton. The situation was deplorable because Altovise was still struggling to harness over $5 million in debt that Sammy had left her. She'd lost the Davis estate and many valuable mementos when they were auctioned in a public sale. Altovise, who'd endured a long battle with alcoholism, had left Sarasota to return to California, only to realize that there was no one there that she could trust.

During the winter of 2008, Altovise often sounded bewildered and disoriented on the phone. I could tell she'd been drinking, and was very depressed. She couldn't understand the motives of the book's author. "He didn't even know me," she kept saying, since he hadn't even arranged to interview her. I felt guilty because I hadn't given Altovise the encouragement she needed to finally speak up about her life. In fact, we'd delayed working on her story because I'd felt she wasn't ready. After seeing the unflattering book, though, I felt that Altovise deserved a chance to be heard. So, I tried to quickly gather the materials needed to finally start her autobiography.

I found my first window of opportunity. I felt comforted in knowing that Grover was in a safe new rehab program, and I could try to put out some of the other fires. First, I'd help Altovise write her memoir. Then, I'd start building our production company. Fires, however, can spread much faster than we'd imagine, and unfortunately, it was too late to contain most of the flames. Altovise died that spring before addressing the controversies that eventually consumed her.

Stunned by her death, I was an emotional wreck. During the following weeks, I felt so torn and confused that I didn't know what to do. Although Grover was expecting me, I didn't come to visit him on the first weekend that he was allowed to have guests. I simply wasn't up to any more pressures. Cell phones weren't allowed at the program, nor were phone calls to the clients, so I left a message that I wasn't coming with one of the supervisors. For some reason, however, he didn't give Grover my message until four days later. During that period, Grover seemed to believe that I'd given up on him and was leaving him.

On Easter Sunday, Grover looked unlike himself, and I noticed tears in his eyes during the service. Even at lunch, he seemed preoccupied with thoughts that were weighing him down. Something was very wrong. When it was time to leave, Grover said he just wanted to come home with me. I was very close to saying, "Just get in," but I didn't, and I'd always regret this.

Instead, we said goodbye.

Grover kissed me and tried to smile. Then, as he hugged my daughter, he told her, "Take good care of your mom for me."

I tried to guard my emotions as I slowly drove off, although a dreadful feeling suddenly crept over me. After all, I'd planned to be back in a few weeks and we'd have more time to talk. I glanced back at Grover, who stood near the driveway as he watched us leave. I remember this very clearly, because it was an exceptional moment. The sun suddenly beamed down on his sunglasses and flashed brilliantly on his parting smile. It was that same dazzling smile that had charmed so many women. But, as we waved this time, I felt a deep and inexplicable sadness.

Two nights later, I found myself crying for no apparent reason, but Grover was on my mind.

The following day, I got the call. Grover was in the intensive care unit of a hospital. As I threw my things in the car, and jumped behind the wheel, I braced myself. I had no idea of what was ahead.

I spent three days, praying by Grover's bedside, hoping that he'd open his eyes. He hadn't responded since he'd had a massive seizure and heart attack, the result of apparently ingesting a lethal dose of antifreeze. Although the doctor's prognosis was grave, I wasn't going to give up on Grover, because I was sure that he could hear me. All he had to do was open his eyes, and they'd give him a few more days to improve.

"Grover," I said, trying to coax him. "You've got to try!"

As the time began to run out, however, I knew he had to prepare to go 'home.' There were so many things I'd longed to share, new revelations that I knew he needed, so I pulled out my Bible and began a crash course.

I urged Grover to reach out to the Holy Spirit, and I held his arm up, to help him. I told him to let go of any angry or hateful thoughts, as well as anything else that could block him. He desperately needed the Spirit, whether he was going to fight for his life, or peacefully go home to heaven.

There was someone from his childhood whom he'd never forgiven for hurting him, and I urged him to finally do so.

"Keep your heart free of any thoughts that can block you," I stressed. "Just think of Jesus and the beauty that's waiting in heaven." I sang, *Amazing Grace,* his favorite hymn, and had a nurse switch the sound system in his room to a Christian radio station.

I told Grover that, if he wanted to live, I'd help him through his recovery. But, if he wanted to go, I understood. I reminded him that Jesus loved him and offered a paradise much better than ours. I told him not to be afraid. He'd been forgiven.

I shared everything I'd learned about the Holy Spirit, and desperately prayed for it to come. And as I cried out to God, I began to sense that something was happening. Although he couldn't speak, I knew that Grover felt it, too. The whole room seemed to be filled with it.

Extraordinary things started to happen. Grover's respiratory machine was increasing flashing the "S" sign. Excitedly, he was breathing on his own. The sign was flashing so rapidly, that the machine started ringing like music.

"It's here, Grover!" I cried out. "Can you feel it?"

Grover not only felt it. I felt sure that he was seeing it.

The euphoria that filled the room was overwhelming, and I was laughing and crying at the same time. "Can't you feel it?" I cried.

We'd longed to experience the Holy Spirit together, and we'd finally shared that magnificent moment.

Then, peacefully, Grover went home.

Despite the blessing of having shared this experience, I still had trouble accepting Grover's death. In fact, a combination of grief and guilt began to overtake me. Several questions kept replaying in my head.

"Why had I put him in that program?"

"What was I thinking?"

"Wasn't it obvious, he was miserable? Why didn't I see the signs?"

It was agonizing, because I couldn't stop asking questions.

"How could this have happened?"

I knew that Grover wanted a new life, and he'd tried hard to change, but like a fish out of water, he'd often been lost. In many ways, I felt responsible for his dilemma. He wanted to be with me, but was caught between two worlds.

Reading some of his last letters again, I noticed a desperate tone in his words. Why hadn't I seen the signs before?

"You are my strength," he'd said, but he'd grown fearful that I would leave him.

The realization of this began to haunt me. How could Grover think that I'd abandon him? I wasn't going to leave him when he needed me most. In his confusion, he must have thought that I'd left him at the program so I could move on with my life. When I realized this, I held my stomach as nausea overtook me. In a high-pitched wail that probably pierced the heavens, I screamed, "I wasn't leaving you!"

On the night prior to Grover's memorial service, when I was trying to find his favorite Bible verse, I was suddenly 'led' to a message in Job 36:15-16. It was a loving and reassuring 'note' from the Lord:

But those who suffer he delivers in their suffering; he speaks to them in their affliction. He is wooing you from the jaws of distress to a spacious place free from restriction, to the comfort of your table laden with choice food.

Instantly, I recalled the vision I'd had a year before, the dream where I'd brought Grover to the 'table' where Jesus sat. I smiled, knowing it was the Lord's sweet way of letting me know that Grover made it there safely.

"Praise God," I cried, joyfully. "Thank you, Jesus!"

On the morning of the service, the Lord also led me to the last entry in Grover's personal journal. There, written from his heart, was his deepest prayer. I knew that, during his last days, he'd reached out to God in an urgent way, and prayed for both of us. The Lord had heard his prayer and responded to his cry.

I had the scripture from Job printed for Grover's memorial service and shared my story about 'the Lord's table' during the eulogy, and I knew that I'd treasure them forever.

Despite these comforting experiences, I had good days and bad, and couldn't seem to find any lasting peace. There were times when I felt angry, but didn't know why. Then, I'd feel guilty about being angry. I wondered how other mourners handled grief. Was it always so painful?

I didn't understand why I was struggling with my faith? Hadn't I seen God's miracles? Shouldn't I have found comfort in knowing that Grover was safe?

I recalled a special memory from the weekend that Grover was baptized. He'd smiled and said, "Well, Pam, you may not have saved all the people you'd hoped to, but at least you saved one person - me."

Pamela Ann Sherrod

I'd smiled back and nodded, because seeing him being baptized was one of my greatest joys. Yet, I felt like I'd come up short and failed God. Where was my ministry? What had I accomplished for anyone other than us? When would our ministry actually get off the ground? Looking back, I should have focused more attention on one particular Bible story. It revolved around a shepherd who had left his large flock of sheep just to go after one lost lamb.

Grover went to heaven, which was no small miracle, but I wondered why he'd gone so soon. He was only fifty-one, and he'd longed to start a brand new life. I promised him that God would show up, and that he could expect to experience powerful miracles. Then, he'd have a testimony that would help other recovering alcoholics. I told him to expect to feel God's presence. But I'd meant, right here on earth. So, what had happened? Had we backslid too far? Had we made too many mistakes? Had we failed to answer the calling that God had put in our hearts?

Why had this happened?

The Bible had always provided me with answers, but when I didn't understand them, I looked toward the church for wisdom. I'd find it at Harvest Tabernacle, in the same sanctuary in which I'd first met Grover. It wasn't during a normal service, however, but on the occasion of another tragic death. An Associate Pastor had committed suicide, and during the funeral service, Pastor Minor spoke of his own pain and frustration, and how he, too, had cried out to God, "Where's the victory in this?"

Yes, I wondered, where is the victory?

He shared the insight he'd gained from the lives of the prophets, Elijah and Elisha. Many amazing wonders were attributed to them. However, the last, supposedly missing miracle actually occurred after Elisha's death. Pastor Minor spoke about the particular moment in which a dead man returned to life after touching Elisha's body. It was a magnificent example of God's ability to restore human life. He pointed out that we try to put God in a neat little box, and demand his performance of various wonders. But, it's always in terms of our limited frame of reference. God, how-

24

ever, is much bigger than that, and his miracles can manifest in ways we'd never expect.

I was comforted by his words, although I was one of the people whom he'd referred to. I'd seen many miracles, but nothing as dramatic as the occurrence recorded in the Bible. So, even though I believed that it happened during biblical times, I found it difficult to imagine it occurring in the present.

Without realizing it, I'd filtered the message to make it more acceptable. I was viewing the story from a contemporary context, especially the notion that a miracle could spring from a disaster. Yes, the more I thought of it, the more convinced I was that we could still see the miracles we'd longed for, but they'd actually manifest in the lives of others. I began to envision a ministry in which we'd launch outreach efforts to help recovering substance abusers. We'd document and showcase the miracle healings of former addicts and support programs that facilitate recovery efforts. This seemed like the perfect answer. I'd channel my sorrow over Grover's loss into a program which would hopefully save others' lives.

Yes, I felt convicted. I'd not only complete the work I'd begun with Altovise, but launch the ministry I'd planned with Grover. Although he was gone, his dream could still be realized. This had to be the answer. It seemed like the most 'natural' thing to do.

The next question was "How?"

I recalled how desperately Grover wanted to see a miracle, and that one of his last desires was to see the film, *The Wrestler.* Its main star, Mickey Rourke, had literally destroyed his life and career, and for many years, no film studio would hire him. Then, finally, one man had enough confidence in him to raise the money for a project. The movie was a success, and Rourke later won Best Actor at the Golden Globe Awards. It was the type of miracle story that Grover could relate to, a true life account of triumph over failure. If Rourke could overcome the odds, then so could he.

So, I'd agreed to go see the film, just as soon as Grover was eligible to leave the rehab program. I still carried the memory of that conversation, because it was one of our last. He died the following week.

Miracle stories had always inspired me, even before I began to witness them. When I was struggling to handle Grover's death, I listened to the testimonies of people who'd experienced miracle healings, and I was strengthened by them. On bad days, I'd pray, read the Scriptures, and spend countless hours watching movies about Jesus, Noah, Joseph and Moses. I began to appreciate, on a completely new level, the importance of inspirational films and documentaries. I realized how vital they were, especially for those who were experiencing tragic losses and other difficult challenges. So, I decided to make this a part of my ministry.

It seemed to make sense when nothing else did. The fact that, both, Altovise and Grover had died from alcoholism–and only thirty-five days apart–held great significance to me. I felt that God had used these tragedies to awaken me to the epidemic problem of addition, and compel me to take action.

I decided to form RisingStar31 to develop inspirational books and films, especially about miracles. And I launched plans to produce a documentary to showcase the testimonies of miracle healings. Some of the messages we gathered were so compelling that I decided to start a website on which to feature them and it was called miraclesandangels.org. The idea was to offer a 24-hour source of hope for people in crisis and in need of support.

In the meantime, I finished editing **The Last Chapter in the Life of Mrs. Sammy Davis, Jr.** and our screenplay, **A Detour to Mexico**. I planned to use the proceeds from the books to finance the work ahead of me. Sometimes, I felt like I was running in circles, and at other times, barely functioning at all, but I kept myself busy. Deep inside, however, I knew something was missing.

What I didn't realize was that I'd left no room for God, or the powerful miracles of his love. I'd been so busy that I failed to see the deeper meaning in the Scriptures. Had I not been forced to stop, I would have also missed the prophetic message tucked in Grover's last letter. I'm thankful to Christ for bringing my attention to the amazing miracle that would slowly be revealed.

It actually began ten days before Grover died, and would continue to unfold, at least, two years after his death. He'd noticed that a strange coincidence had occurred, and he recorded it that same day in the letter he mailed. It surrounded an interesting book he'd read and shared with me while I was visiting. He thought it was called *The Wife of His Youth,* and it was a love story about an African-American couple who'd been enslaved prior to the Civil War. Somehow, they'd been separated during the months following their emancipation, and for many years they'd searched, but couldn't find one another. The wife, who'd never given up, finally found him twenty-five years later, just one day prior to the date he'd planned to remarry.

Grover and I were touched by this narrative, especially by the man's acceptance of his wife after all those years.

"Would you have done that?" I asked. He slowly smiled and replied, "It would be a hard decision."

Then, in the letter I received from him a few days later, he included an update:

"This is wild: When I went to quiet time this morning I was turning to Matthew, but I opened the Bible to Malachi. I began to read there and in the second chapter and fifteenth verse it says 'no man should act treacherously toward *the wife of his youth.*'"

Referring back to the story he'd read, he mentioned that the author was Charles Chestnut, and his book was actually called *The Wife of His Youth and other Stories of the Color Line.*

After reading Grover's letter, I decided to read the scripture he'd mentioned, and when I opened to the verse in Malachi, I immediately noticed something else:

Has not the LORD made them one? In flesh and spirit they are his. And why one? Because he was seeking godly offspring. So guard yourself in your spirit, and do not break faith with the wife of your youth.

For a moment, I felt alarmed by the strong wording. As a couple, we'd initially struggled with issues of sin and infidelity. However, we'd become engaged and were devoted to building a strong

Christian marriage. We wanted to serve and be faithful to God, and to each other. Did this, somehow, have a deeper meaning?

I began to wonder if Grover had read the material I'd left with him. On Easter, just before departing, I'd handed him a copy of *A Detour to Mexico.* I was anxious to know if he'd liked it. Oddly enough, the plot was similar to the story he'd shared. When I wrote it, I was inspired by a beautiful verse from Song of Songs? The scripture was different from other Bible verses. It was based on a love story and the quest of separated lovers who were searching for one another. Grover, who loved to read, always delivered the most amazing critiques on books. So, I couldn't wait to hear his views.

The following week, when I picked up Grover's belongings from the farm, I inquired to find out if he'd had a chance to read the screenplay. However, no one knew.

Back then, I didn't focus much attention on this memory. Instead, I became so busy with my projects that it rarely came to mind. I didn't perceive the miracle that was unfolding. It didn't begin to occur to me until I heard the word, "Stop."

"Stop?" I whispered, in dismay. The timing couldn't have been worse. I'd finally published the screenplay, *A Detour to Mexico,* and fulfilled a long awaited dream. I'd also planned a promotional trip to New York, and looked forward to distributing the first copies of the book.

Back in 2005, when Altovise and I first created the screenplay, I'd fallen in love with the characters and couldn't wait to bring them to life on the silver screen. Friends had also enjoyed the story, including a Disney Channel producer and a star from *The Cosby Show.* They thought we had a smash hit on our hands. Apparently, someone else did, as well. An extremely popular film was produced with a story line so identical to ours, that an attorney confirmed that it had too many striking similarities to be coincidental. Unknowingly, I'd put the script right in their hands.

After our screenplay was stolen we experienced years of painful setbacks and tragedies, but I'd finally published the book version of our story. Now, the world would finally meet our amazing characters. I was so thrilled that I could almost hear Etta James' hit, *At Last,* playing in my ear.

Instead, however, I'd heard the word "Stop!"

Admittedly, it was painful to engage the brakes, especially since I'd invested so much into the book. However, it was the wrong time to launch it. God was calling me to handle something far more important–the assignment I'd been dodging. So, I put a hold on the promotional plans for both of my books.

Instead, while in New York, I spent considerable time in prayer. I remembered that Pastor Scott, whose church I attended, urged me to pause for a season and "recharge." He reminded me that, even Jesus had taken some time away from people, so that he could be with God. "How can you serve others well, if you don't?" he asked.

That day, I hadn't fully appreciated his wisdom. Yet, as the weeks passed, I made greater efforts to study the Bible more closely. I desperately needed to know God's will for my life, and honor it.

After months of prayer, I realized that I'd been led to Isaiah 43 and the other Bible passages for a specific reason. They revealed something extraordinary about God, and the power of his love. I'd been a witness to his miracles, and although I didn't have all the answers, I certainly knew what I'd seen. With a deep breath, I pulled out my laptop, knowing God had revealed a message which was far more important than my fears about delivering it.

Chapter Three: God Really Loves You

For God so loved the world that he gave his one and only Son that
whoever believes in him shall not perish but have eternal life.
John 3:16

When I first believed that I'd heard from my fiancé, I needed proof that it really was him. After all, every journalist has in-
grained training to research a situation before making any judg-
ments. Since I was still adjusting to the shock of Grover's death, I
had to consider the possibility that I was hallucinating.

At first, the occurrences were very subtle. I began noticing
that some of Grover's things were out of place. I'd brought his
belongings home from the hospital and his bags from the rehab
program, and I thought I'd absentmindedly left a few items in the
wrong place.

Then, there were other peculiar incidents, but they didn't
seem monumental. Like, when the lights suddenly went out, and
the water started running in the utility room. I made a few jokes
about it, because of their increasing frequency.

The first powerful encounter, however, took place in my car.
I was driving down the highway, remembering some special times
I'd spent with Grover, when I began to feel melancholy. I realized
how much I missed him, and sighed, "I still love you."

I'd barely gotten the words out, when I felt a sudden wave of
love rush over me. No one touched me, physically, and yet, it felt
like Grover had hugged me. No words can describe that moment,
but there was a different energy in the car, and it was so powerful
and exuberant that it was unmistakable. I knew Grover's aura, and
without a doubt, I recognized his presence. And he wasn't alone. It
felt like, both, Grover and Jesus were right there with me.

This happened again, only a few hours later, but I was meeting with students and it was extremely awkward. I started gig-

gling, and when I tried to regain my composure, it was nearly impossible. I remember whispering, "Please, not here. The children are here!"

To be honest, I was thrilled by the occurrence but unsure of what to make of it.

To my amazement, I actually saw Grover one evening. While I was sleeping, I had a brief vision that we were hugging each other. Then, we suddenly flew straight through my window and up into the evening sky.

It would happen again. On the second occasion, we embraced and effortlessly soared right through the bedroom ceiling. I was sure we were in heaven, because I remember feeling happy to be there with him. He didn't speak, but he looked amazing. His smile was radiant and I'd never seen him look so joyful. I was totally unafraid, and never worried that he'd drop me. In fact, it felt like we were weightless and suspended in air. Although, I felt lightheaded and giddy, I still remembered my responsibilities back at home. The last thing I recall was laughing and saying, "I've got to go back."

During the following days, I wondered if I'd simply been dreaming. I was very spiritual and I'd documented numerous miracles, but I'd never seen anything of this nature.

The third sighting was very different. It occurred right after I'd suffered a major blow. I'd made an error while taking a computerized exam. I'd pushed the button to end the test before I'd completed all the questions. When I realized my mistake, I was so distraught, I could barely speak. I came home in tears and went straight to bed.

Suddenly, I saw Grover sitting across the room, even though there was no chair in the area. He looked different, somewhat stiff, and not as solid as before. In fact, I could almost see through him. This was the first time, however, that he actually spoke.

"Why are you worrying about that, anyway?" He asked. "You should be working on the book."

I straightened up.

"Alright," I responded, feeling somewhat better. I assumed that he was talking about Altovise's story. I felt an increase in my energy level and pulled myself together. Yes, I'd finish editing the book and get it published. When I dried my face, Grover was gone.

Looking back, I'd probably made a second error. I don't think Grover was referring to Altovise's story. I believe he was talking about 'ours.'

Back then, I also assumed that he'd come back for similar visits. When he didn't, I wondered where he'd gone. Weeks would pass, and I wouldn't feel his presence. Then, suddenly, there would be a clear sign that he'd returned. After a while, I began to notice a pattern.

Whenever I was angry and feeling considerably less spiritual, he seemed to be missing. When I spent more time in prayer and nurtured a more loving heart, he seemed to be everywhere. No one had a sense of humor like Grover's, so I recognized some of the humorous devices he used to confirm that he was with me.

I began to think of him as my special guardian angel, because he seemed to be trying to help me. I'd casually ask a question, and sometimes, within hours, the answer would appear. It reminded me of the experiences I'd had during prayer time, when I'd pray about an issue, then see it mentioned directly in the Bible. I'd visit a new church, and the pastor would speak as though he knew me. Despite all of my mistakes, God was still guiding me. For years, I'd found his messages tucked in books and magazines and often in the most unexpected places. Now, there was something special he was revealing, and it had something to do with Grover.

There were days when I'd step into a store, or turn on a radio, and suddenly hear a love song written with a special message. From old classics to contemporary hits, from Phil Collins to Beyoncé, the messages kept coming. I was especially moved by a lovely CD recorded by Josh Groban. Even the songs rendered in different languages seemed to be telling our story.

One day, I was stunned when I spotted a music video produced by Black Eyed Peas. They were a group I'd rarely listened

Pamela Ann Sherrod

to, which my daughter felt was due to my age. **Meet Me Halfway** was the name of their song, and after watching the entire video, I knew it wasn't by happenstance that I'd found it. The words and imagery expressed a love story about the plight of a couple who were separated by different realms. To be reunited, they had to cross the galaxies to find one another, and both asked, "Can you meet me halfway?"

"That's it!" I realized. That was the universal question.

Was Grover trying to tell me it was possible?

"But, how?" I asked. "How is it done?"

Being a journalist, I began to research the question. As always, the Bible was my first stop.

What I uncovered was very eye-opening. The spirit realm was very real, but if one wasn't careful they could be lured toward the wrong place. At first, I was very confused. Although, the Lord had assured me that Grover was in heaven, I was growing concerned about his motives. I'd started reading other books about the afterlife, and I generally understood that good spirits moved up higher toward God, while the troubled spirits hung around the earth. So, what condition was Grover's soul or spirit in?

Admittedly, I became a bit guarded. I remember praying about this, and asking Grover (if present) to join me in confessing that Jesus is our Lord and Savior. Just to be extra careful, a few days later, I said, "I love you, but if you're not here with God's blessing, and operating IN Christ, I rebuke you. You can't stay here. And if you're not in the right place, I urge you to go to 'the light.'" Then, I prayed that he'd go to the light.

I have to admit, however, that like many people who'd lost a loved one, there was a natural temptation to consult a psychic. But, God had told me to warn young people to stay away from the occult, and the Bible warned against consulting with mediums. In fact, in very strong language recorded in Deuteronomy 18:10-12, it was written:

34

Let no one be found among you who . . . practices divination or sorcery, interprets omens, engages in witchcraft, or casts spells or is a medium or spiritualist or who consults the dead.

So, hiring a psychic was not an option. Nor, was I to make any attempts to reach out and contact Grover.

I continued reading the Bible and several other books, realizing how little I really knew about this realm. I found stories of people who'd been reunited with their deceased loved ones and published studies by physicians who'd documented cases of near death experiences. I read books on various theories of death and dying, and counselor's guides on grief and healing. I looked closely at their conclusions, and was amazed.

There were striking similarities between the things I'd witnessed and those which were documented. I stayed up late many nights, just to read the accounts, and I cried with joy, because I'd found others who'd shared similar experiences. I wasn't alone, after all. And, I hadn't gone crazy.

Still, I needed some guidance about how to 'behave' with Grover. I knew he was near, but I didn't know how to communicate without committing a sin. Further research led me to the study of astral travel. Through this method, people could place themselves in trance-like states of mind, which allowed them to take out-of-body trips. As intriguing as it was, I decided to do a little more research, and I discovered that the Bible warned against this, too.

"Sorry, Baby..." I whispered. "I can't meet you that way."

So, I prayed to God for more wisdom. I didn't want to offend the Lord, but I longed to know how Grover was really doing. We'd both experienced the fullness of the Holy Spirit before he died, and God had been kind in letting me know that Grover was with him. But the truth was, I still missed him.

"How can we communicate?" I asked.

In a sudden flurry of events, I felt that Grover was leading me to the answer. It began when I got a strange call on my cell phone from a woman in Georgia. She was trying to contact a local church known as Victory at Sarasota, where Grover and I had briefly attended. When asked how she happened to phone me, she mentioned that she'd watched their church service on a cable program, and had taken down their phone number. But, instead, she'd reached me.

Having been reminded of the church, I decided to attend their next service. Somehow, I sensed that a message was awaiting me. Pastor Gibbs' sermon was based on a wonderful theme, and in summary it meant, "Where your heart is, that's where your life is." I was further intrigued when he mentioned the importance of getting to the 'cleft' in the high place.

I was pretty sure that I'd read about this in Song of Songs. In fact, I'd been so inspired by that particular passage, that I'd actually used an excerpt from it while writing **A Detour to Mexico.** I knew a little about its history and the spiritual implications of where the 'high place' (or mountainside) was. I just wasn't sure of the route required to reach it.

"How do I get there?" I whispered.

During the following days, I felt sure that Grover was directing me.

"Draw closer to God," was the message I heard. "Do whatever it takes to get closer to God."

I opened the Bible and took a closer look at the second chapter of Song of Songs. What had initially drawn me to the verse? Was there something else there that I hadn't noticed? I studied the words again.

My dove in the clefts of the rock, in the hiding places of the mountainside, show me your face, let me hear your voice; for your voice is sweet, and your face is lovely. Catch for us the foxes, the little foxes that ruin the vineyards, our vineyards that are in bloom.

Again, I wondered if Grover had read our screenplay before he died and noticed the connection to this scripture.

I recalled from a Bible study, that "little foxes" meant the elements in our lives which separated us from God. These included doubt, hate and unforgiveness. We had to be set free from all these things to experience the fullness of God's loving Spirit, and the miracles that followed.

Without fully realizing it, I'd tried to convey this same message in our screenplay. The theme would later be used as the motto for my ministry work: *"God is love...so, whatever you do...whatever you create, do it with love."*

Was Grover now leading me back to this same message? Or, was it just another strange coincidence?

I heard once more, "Get closer to God."

As the months passed, I became very busy with new projects, and one day I realized that my heart had finally healed. I didn't think of Grover quite as often as before, and I began to question whether I'd actually seen him.

"Maybe the visions were due to shock or trauma," I said, trying to rationalize.

"But, had I simply imagined him?"

It's funny, how the word, *imagine*, would later spark a 'supernatural conversation' that would change my views about life, death, heaven and earth.

It began one day while I was on the way to The Church of Hope.

It was a lovely Sunday morning, but as I drove along the highway I felt extremely depressed. Sundays were often difficult. They were the days when I missed Grover the most. There were so many memories to deal with, as most of our 'dates' had revolved around church functions.

I felt lonely going to services without him, especially to such a large congregation. I was new to the Church of Hope, but I was guessing that their membership was close to 1,500 people. It was a relatively new, state-of-the-art building, with a 15-story steeple and 56-foot long stained glass window featuring the word HOPE. With its attractive architecture and compelling signage, no traveler driving along U.S. Highway 75 could miss it.

As it came into view, I wondered if Grover would have liked the church. He was actually the first person who'd mentioned it to me, and that was back when the building was still under construction. He'd apparently worked a few days with the con-

Pamela Ann Sherrod

tractor who'd installed the floors, and he'd been impressed with the designs, but hadn't said much more.

I'd recently decided to join the church, but I was still so new that I didn't quite feel at home, yet. As I drove by, I glanced at the impressive steeple, towering over the highway. How commanding it was, especially at night, with its pyramid shaped roof and translucent lighting effects. Its interior features were just as striking.

I suddenly recalled a wooden crucifix that Grover had helped erect. It stood beside an outreach mission located just across town. When it came to visiting the various congregations in Sarasota, we'd certainly made the rounds, and even after church-hopping for four years, we still hadn't agreed upon the right one.

Would he have joined this new church with me? I wondered.

"What do you think of it, baby?" I asked, as though he were sitting beside me.

I took the next exit and maneuvered down the ramp. Then, just as I approached the light at the bottom, I 'felt' what seemed to be a reply. At first, I thought I was mistaken. However, I realized it was Grover.

Of course, it wasn't the first time that I'd sensed his presence, nor was it the first time he'd ever spoken, but it was the first time he'd ever communicated in this manner. He was speaking to me, but not exactly with his voice. It was through some type of internal thought process. What was stunning, though, was that he'd not only heard my question, but somehow known my thoughts.

Grover assured me that he'd be right beside me at church, and not to be depressed, because I wasn't alone. I clearly understood what he was telling me, and as I turned onto Fruitville Road, the dialogue continued.

I asked if it was really he who was communicating. He assured me that it was, and that we'd be together during the service, just as we'd always been.

"But, I can't fully appreciate that you're there," I said, "since I can't see your face or hold your hand."

38

"Then, imagine that I'm there," he responded.

At that moment, with the word 'imagine' still dangling in my head, I started to make a left turn, when I noticed something about the car ahead of me. There, on its license plate was the word, *"Imagine."*

Stunned, I softly laughed at the 'coincidence.'

"So, you are here!" I said.

Grover confirmed this.

"So, we can communicate this way?" I asked. "But, how do I distinguish between your thoughts and mine? We can't have a spontaneous discussion or even a decent argument, if you already know what I'm thinking."

I didn't mean to complain, but it was a little startling.

"Wow!" I whispered. In God's realm, they even knew our thoughts.

Although, I hadn't had time to fully process this, it explained a number of scriptures I'd read, as well as numerous experiences I'd had.

On some level, I immediately realized that I'd have to censor my thoughts. This, I should have been practicing, anyway, since God knew them all. But, what was most amazing was that we could communicate. When I had more time, I'd try to figure out the details.

Communication, though, had always been a two-way-street. At least, it was for me. So, how would I speak with someone who was omnipresent, and already knew all my thoughts? How would he derive any pleasure, with so little spontaneity?

"It can't be too much fun for you," I said, " ... if you already know what I'm thinking. What thoughts are yours? And what are actually mine?

"What does it matter?" he replied. "They're *ours*."

"Ours?" I asked. It was too confusing for me to fully grasp, and I didn't have enough time, anyway. I'd just reached the church.

A few minutes later, Darla, Pastor Scott's wife, stepped onto the front podium and stood beside her husband. She had a sweet and nurturing spirit, and usually offered the opening remarks.

Sometimes, she became very touched while delivering a message and such would be the case that morning.

Darla had a special experience to share about a miracle that had occurred. One of the church members had gone to a beach at Siesta Key, which was located just across the bridge from Sarasota. With its sugar-like sand and lovely views, it was considered the country's most popular beach and it was a well-known tourist destination.

While walking along the shore, the woman looked down and happened to notice two large attractive sea shells. She picked them up and found something written on the back of each one. She was amazed by the words and felt sure that they represented a message from God. On the shells were written, "Hope" and "Joy."

The woman brought the shells to Darla, as she was also certain that they were meant for her. Not only was their congregation known as The Church of Hope, but she knew that the words 'Hope' and 'Joy' were printed on Darla's license plate.

As Darla finished her story, I began to feel lightheaded. This amazing event, like so many others, had God's signature written all over it. Less than ten minutes earlier, I'd seen a stunning example of God's miraculous power, confirmed on a license plate. Now, here was another confirmation on a license plate, that, indeed, with God, all things were possible.

This experience became more precious when I later recalled that Grover had always noticed little things. He'd stop to watch a bird bringing food to her young, or leap from the car to examine a favorite plant. He often commented on clever messages he noticed on signs, private boats, and other things that I usually missed. We both, however, were intrigued by something that repeatedly occurred during the last year of his life. Increasingly, while we were driving, Grover would spot words printed on license plates that echoed the very things we were discussing. He thought it was an odd coincidence, but I half-jokingly remarked, "See, the miracles are already starting." How strange it was, that I'd forgotten this. Grover obviously hadn't.

During the 2010 Christmas season, I sent a holiday card to the Pastor and his wife, and enclosed a letter in which I shared with them this special experience. I wanted them to know that 'Darla's miracle' had touched more lives than she was aware of.

Still, I marveled at how it had happened. What type of power did God possess, that he could weave all of these events through strangers' lives and orchestrate everything so magnificently? How could the details prophesized so long ago, unfold and have an impact on our contemporary lives? The beautiful passages in Song of Songs spoke of it, and revealed one of the keys to living a 'supernatural' life. We have to catch the "little foxes" by removing the sin, hatred and unbelief that can effectively block us from God and his wisdom. From numerous other passages in the Bible, I've learned that the age-old mysteries are revealed to those who search for them through and in the Spirit of God.

"God is truly awesome!" I whispered. So is his Word.

I'd been a Christian for many years, yet this event led to a true awakening. From this experience, I'd be blessed with new revelations from the Bible. One of the most precious gifts was my new perspective about life, the death of the body, and the return of the soul to heaven. Now, I've seen proof that, through Christ, we have redemption and eternal life, and IN him, spirits and angels in heaven and believers here on earth work together to fulfill God's perfect will. I know that God's desire is for us to know and operate in his Truth.

I've had the joy of sharing Grover's miracle, as well as my own, and celebrating the gift of eternal life that he's found IN Christ. Now, I know why this particular 'lost lamb' was so important to God's plan.

I'm a witness to the fact that God is real. His prophetic Word is alive, and when one studies and lives by his Word, there is supernatural wisdom and power. God is love, and his love is eternal. It knows no boundaries in heaven or earth, and it defeats even death.

I thank God for providing this extraordinary glimpse of his heavenly realm.

Pamela Ann Sherrod

It's my prayer that you, too, can experience similar miracles in your life, and the magnificent displays of the Lord's amazing love. Without a doubt, it will change your life for eternity.

God bless you.

Psalm 78:2-4

I will utter hidden things, things from of old—
what we have heard and known, what our fathers have told us.
We will not hide them from their children.
We will tell the next generation the praiseworthy deeds of
the LORD, his power, and the wonders he has done.

Concluding Prayer

If you would like to ask Jesus Christ into your life,
this is an opportunity to do so. Simply repeat this
prayer and let it touch your heart and your life:

Father, God,
I repent and ask for forgiveness of my sins,
I forgive those who have wronged me, and hurt me;
I believe in Your Son, Jesus Christ; that he was born
and lived on earth; that he was crucified and
died so that my sins could be forgiven.
I believe that he descended into hell, and rose again,
and that he sits at Your right hand in heaven.
I believe in the Holy Ghost, and ask for the
free gift of the Holy Spirit.
I want to be born again in Christ.

In Jesus' Name. Amen

Thank You

*Thank you for supporting our work. Proceeds from the sale of this book will help us develop programs such as **The Witness to Miracles and Angels** web show and inspirational books, videos and documentaries that celebrate the gift of God's grace.*

For more information, please visit:
www.pamelasherrodministries.org
www.miraclesandangels.org